Ladybug, Ladybug

and
Other Favorite Poems

Cricket Books

Chicago, Illinois

Artists

Cover, Dagmar Fehlau; *Ladybug, Ladybug,* Joan Paley; *Poodle Doodles,* Matt Smith; *Spring Wiggler,* Sharron O'Neil; *The Box,* Lynne Cravath; *A Doggie Song,* Tony Ross; *Ocean Sandwich,* John Sandford; *Sandcastle,* G. Brian Karas; *Knees,* D. Brent Burkett; *Baby Squirrels,* Siri Weber Feeney; *Caterpillar,* P. A. Lewis; *Changes,* Ingrid Slyder; *Limbo Lizards,* Jennifer Hewitson; *Artist,* John Sandford; *Solitary Crocodile,* Brian Lies; *Mushrooms from Heaven,* Sylvia Long; *Ocean Lullaby,* Omar Rayyan; *Bug in the Tub,* Brian Hendrickson; *Snowballs,* Joung Un Kim; *Mariachi Rattlesnake,* Jon Goodell; *Stay, Little Stray,* Gavin Rowe; *Firefly,* Tae-Eun Yoo.

Grateful acknowledgment is made to the following for permission to reprint the copyrighted material listed below.

Jean Hansen-Novak for *Poodle Doodles,* © 2003 by Jeanne Novak.
Carole Gerber for *Spring Wiggler,* © 2003 by Carole Gerber.
Sharon Wooding for *The Box,* © 2002 by Sharon L. Wooding.
Carol A. Grund for *Sandcastle,* © 2004 by Carol A. Grund.
Cheri Smolich for *Baby Squirrels,* © 2004 by Cheryl Smolich.
Virginia Kroll for *Changes,* © 2004 by Virginia Kroll.
Lynne Berry for *Limbo Lizards,* © 2004 by Lynne Berry.
Susan Meyer for *Artist,* © 2003 by Susan Meyer.
Barbara Kerley for *Solitary Crocodile,* © 2003 by Barbara Kelly.
Cynthia Porter for *Ocean Lullaby,* © 2005 by Cynthia Porter.
Carol Samuelson-Woodson for *Bug in the Tub,* © 2002 by Carol Samuelson-Woodson.
Pat Sandifer Borum for *Snowballs,* © 2003 by Pat Sandifer Borum.
Kathy Duval for *Mariachi Rattlesnake,* © 2005 by Kathy Duval.
Dave Crawley for *Stay, Little Stray,* © 2003 by David A. Crawley.
Cathy Cronin for *Firefly,* © 2005 by Cathy Cronin.

These poems first appeared in LADYBUG® magazine.

The Library of Congress Cataloging-in-Publication data for *Ladybug, Ladybug* is available at http://catalog.loc.gov.

Ladybug, Ladybug

Ladybug, Ladybug,
I beg your pardon,
Would you please come
And play in my garden?

Come take a sip
Of the sweet morning dew
That sits on soft petals
Just waiting for you.

For lunch there are aphids
And other fine dishes—
Sweet treats to please you,
All so delicious.

I think you'll enjoy
The evening perfume
As you curl up inside
The bed of a bloom.

—Charles Ghigna

Poodle Doodles

Draw, draw,
Doodle, doodle,
I can make
A curly poodle.

Draw, draw,
Scribble, scribble.
Now I'll make
A bone to nibble!

—*Jean Hansen-Novak*

Spring Wiggler

Twisting,
turning,
left and
right,
the
earthworm
burrows
out of
sight.

In,
out,
up,
down.
It
wiggles
winter
from
the
ground.

Over,
under,
watch
it go,
plowing
dirt
so plants
can
grow.

—Carole Gerber

The Box

When Dad brought home the great big box
And left it by my door,
I crawled inside a cardboard cave
And roared a dragon's roar.

Then one day Daddy carved a litt
Hole into the box.
The cave became a fox's den,
And I became a fox.

Still later I drew flowers on
The cardboard, and a tree.
Dad cut some doors and windows out,
And now I'm being me.

—*Sharon Wooding*

A Doggie Song

Mommy plays the piano,
Fido sings along.
It isn't really singing.
He doesn't know the song.

—*Shirley Anderson*

Ocean Sandwich

They say the ocean's filled with food,
From sea to shining sea.
There's something called a jellyfish,
How tasty can that be?

Before I get my knife and bread,
Before I get my dish,
Can anybody help me find
The peanut butter fish?

—Alan Watson

Sandcastle

Soft and squishy, wet and brown—
Scoop the sand and pack it down.
Fill a bucket, fill a cup,
Dump it out, then build it up.
Here a tower, there a wall,
Now a moat surrounds it all.
Gather sticks to make a gate,
Shells and stones to decorate.
Waves reach up and lick the shore,
Knocking at our castle door.
Soon it all will melt away . . .
Come and build another day!

—Carol A. Grund

Knees

When you are three, "Like me!" said Louise,
You see an awful lot of knees.
Some are knobby, some are thin,
Some are dimpled, and some—*ouch!*—skinned.
Some knees are covered up in dirt.
Some knees hide under Grandma's skirt.
Knees peek out of the holes in jeans,
And gardeners' knees are colored in greens!
"You have knees, too," said Louise, who's three.
"To find them, just do like me.
Bend over and over and magically,
You will see your own two knees!"

—Virginia Nemmers

Baby Squirrels

I see two baby squirrels
Playing in a tree,
Leaping on the branches,
But not too cautiously.
They're learning from their mother
All the things they need to know,
To gather food and stay away
From dangers down below.

—Cheri Smolich

Caterpillar

A brown caterpillar
Crawled up on my shoe.
I stood still and watched
To see what he would do.

He must have thought I was
A stick in his way:
He crawled off again
Without stopping to play!

—*Edith E. Cutting*

Changes

Time for pants and sweatshirts with long sleeves.
Hear me crunch through crackly crimson leaves.
Mums like sunbeams burst in brilliant gold.
Pumpkins grow too plump for me to hold.
Tasty apple cider for us all,
Bonfires, hayrides;
What's the season? FALL!

—*Virginia Kroll*

Limbo Lizards

Limbo Lizards on the loose
Limbo past the barnyard goose.
Goose calls *squawk!*
Lizards rock.
Waggle goose joins wiggle walk.

Lizards jive in jolly jigs,
Limbo past the barnyard pigs.
Pink pigs blink.
Lizards link.
Pig toes tap to cowbell clink.

Limbo Lizards leave the hogs,
Limbo past the barnyard dogs.
Barn pups *yip!*
Lizards dip.
Puppies pounce, one does a flip.

Lizards leap from puppy heap,
Limbo past the barnyard sheep.
Baa! says lamb.
Lizards jam.
Shaggy sheep waltzes with ram.

Limbo Lizards dodge the rats,
Limbo past the barnyard cats.
Barn cats stare.
Lizards pair.
Kittens strut, tails tap the air.

Limbo Lizards steer a course,
Limbo past the barnyard horse.
Horse cries *neigh!*
Lizards sway.
Limbo Lizards groove away.

—*Lynne Berry*

Artist

There's red paint in my hair,
And on my cheek a dab of pink.
The orange on my elbow
Didn't wash off in the sink.
Some green dripped on my foot,
And there's a blue-and-yellow swoop—
When I get in the bath tonight,
I'll make a rainbow soup!

—Susan Meyer

Solitary Crocodile

Solitary crocodile,
Cruising down the river Nile,
Never even stops to smile
But oozes on his way.

Doesn't speak to fish or bird,
Acts as if he hasn't heard,
Doesn't say a single word,
Won't give the time of day!

Won't you stay and chat awhile,
Dark, mysterious crocodile?

—Barbara Kerley

Mushrooms from Heaven

Along the garden path,
Like parasols from heaven,
Mushrooms magically appear.
This year I counted seven.

Silver, gold, white, and tan,
They stand as in a trance,
Providing shade for a parade
Of busy little ants.

—*Charles Ghigna*

Ocean Lullaby

On lapping waves, silvery starshine will slide.
Safe in warm tide pools, starfish will glide.
The moon will roll overhead, silver and bright.
Dolphins will leap through the waves in its light.
All night, while the moon and the stars wheel along,
The ocean will rock to the whale's sweet song.
And as I sleep snugly all night in my bed,
Dreams of the ocean will sing in my head.

—Cynthia Porter

Bug in the Tub

A beetle bug
Waits in the tub
When I'm ready
For a scrub.
Is he dirty,
Do you think?
Is he hoping
For a drink?
Does he want
To take a swim?
Think I'll leave it
Up to him.
I'll skip my bath.
If he's like me,
He'll want to have
Some privacy!

—*Carol Samuelson-Woodson*

Snowballs

When snow falls,
And cold winds blow,
Snowballs
Are fun to throw.

Scoop some snow
From the ground.
Roll it. Pat it.
Make it round.

Winter snowballs,
Throw them high.
Watch them fall—
Watch them fly!

—*Pat Sandifer Borum*

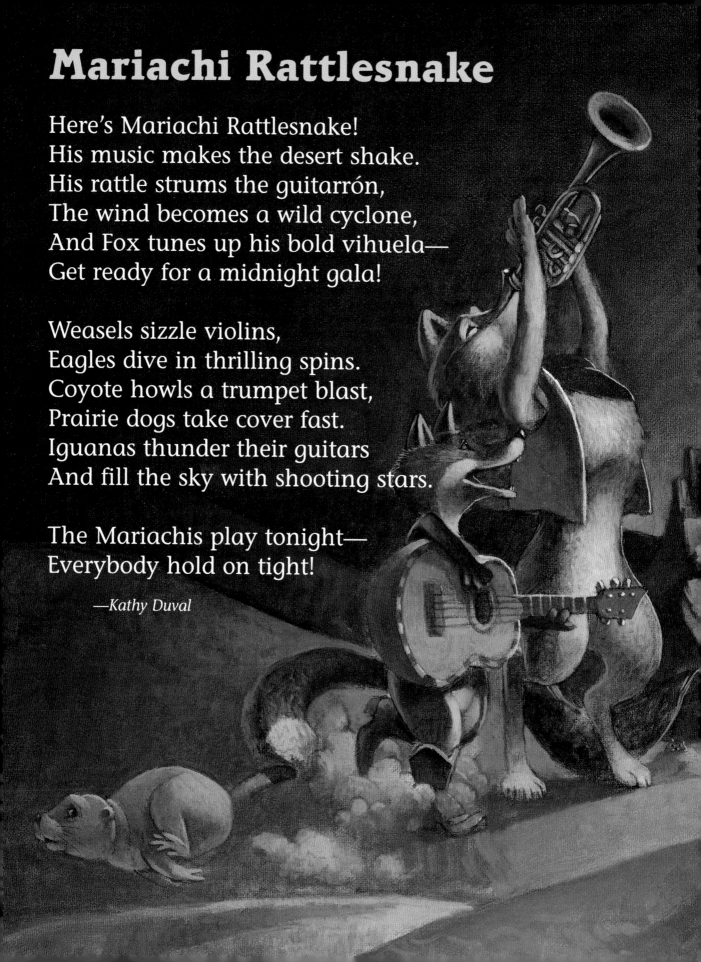

Mariachi Rattlesnake

Here's Mariachi Rattlesnake!
His music makes the desert shake.
His rattle strums the guitarrón,
The wind becomes a wild cyclone,
And Fox tunes up his bold vihuela—
Get ready for a midnight gala!

Weasels sizzle violins,
Eagles dive in thrilling spins.
Coyote howls a trumpet blast,
Prairie dogs take cover fast.
Iguanas thunder their guitars
And fill the sky with shooting stars.

The Mariachis play tonight—
Everybody hold on tight!

—Kathy Duval

Stay, Little Stray

Stay, little stray. Don't go away.
You look so hungry and thin.
Don't be shy. No need to cry.
Don't be afraid to come in.

Here is a dish. Eat as you wish.
No need to forage and roam.
I'm stroking your fur, hearing you purr.
Tiger, you just found a home!

—*Dave Crawley*

Firefly

Firefly, firefly, glowing bright,
Lighting up my room tonight,
I wish you'd stay till morning's light—
Or at least until I'm sleeping tight.

—*Cathy Cronin*